Groping
Toward the Light

OTHER BOOKS BY DARRELL SCHWEITZER

NOVELS
The White Isle
The Shattered Goddess
The Mask of the Sorcerer

COLLECTIONS AND STORY-CYCLES
We Are All Legends
Tom O'Bedlam's Night Out
Transients
Refugees from an Imaginary Country
Necromancies and Netherworlds (with Jason Van Hollander)
Nightscapes
The Great World and the Small (forthcoming)
Echoes of the Goddess (forthcoming)
Sekenre: The Book of the Sorcerer (forthcoming)

POETRY AND LIGHT VERSE
Non Compost Mentis
Poetica Dementia
Stop Me Before I Do It Again!

NON-FICTION
The Dream Quest of H.P. Lovecraft
Pathways to Elfland: The Writings of Lord Dunsany
Lord Dunsany: A Bibliography (with S.T. Joshi)
SF Voices (interviews)
SF Voices 1 (interviews)
SF Voices 5 (interviews)
Speaking of Horror (interviews)
Windows of the Imagination
On Writing Science Fiction: The Editors Strike Back
(with George Scithers and John M. Ford)

AS EDITOR
Discovering H.P. Lovecraft
Exploring Fantasy Worlds
The Ghosts of the Heaviside Layer by Lord Dunsany
Discovering Modern Horror Fiction (2 vols)
Discovering Stephen King
Discovering Classic Horror Fiction
Discovering Classic Fantasy
Tales from the Spaceport Bar (with George Scithers)
Another Round at the Spaceport Bar (with George Scithers)

"Through life and death both, we are groping toward the light."

—EDWARD PICKMAN DERBY

Groping Toward the Light

Poems for
Midnight and After
by
DARRELL SCHWEITZER

With illustrations by
Jason Van Hollander

WILDSIDE PRESS

❖

BERKELEY HEIGHTS, NJ • 2000

Most of the poems in this book have been previously published in
magazines, including:

*Weird Tales, Fosfax, Ash-Wing, Eldritch Tales, Dreams and Nightmares,
Star-Line, Fantasy Tales, Amazing Stories, Lore, The Lynx, Tomorrow And....,
Dark Regions, Mythlore, The Silver Web, Midnight Shambler, Crypt of Cthulhu,
Deathrealm, Weirdbook Supplement, Tales from the Cthulhu Codex,
Grue, Pirate Writings*

Published in 2000 in the United States of America by
Wildside Press, 522 Park Avenue, Berkeley Heights, New Jersey 07922
http://www.wildsidepress.com

Book design and illustrations © 2000 by Jason Van Hollander

Paperback edition ISBN 1-58715-109-X
Hardcover edition ISBN 1-58715-108-1

TABLE OF CONTENTS

Introduction, by Donald Sidney-Fryer xiii

APPARITIONS FAINTLY SEEN

He Unwraps Himself. 1
Each Evening Emily Dreamed of the Grave 3
The Skeptics 5
I Know That I Have Slept with the Dead 7
I Want to Be a Vampire. 9
What if the Dead Are Laughing? 10
I am the Ghost. 11
Heretical Gospel 13
Two Knights 14
Invocation 18
After the Night 20
Let Me Glide Gently Into My Death 22
Still There 25
The Houseguest's Ghost Story 27
The Man in the Wind 29

Old Father Stone 32
The Wizard's Glass 34
Mad Song the First 36
Not Your Typical Horror Poem. 38
It Wasn't Haunted 39
Death's Favorite Snapshot 41

HISTORY AND OTHER ENIGMAS

Concerning the Fate of Philip,
Emissary of Pope Alexander III to Prester John 44
The Truth About Caspar Hauser. 48
The Lost Dauphins 50
Another Enigma. 55
The Shipwreck. 57
The Outcast. 59
Roman Coins. 62
Signs and Portents. 65
Romulus Augustulus Deposed 67
Byzantine Portraits:
    I   *Heraclius in Constantinople* 70
    II   *Heraclius in Persia* 72
    III   *Heraclius in Jerusalem* 75
    IV   *Justinian the Second Rages* 77
    V   *Theodosius the Third*. 80
    VI   *Michael VIII* 82
    VII *Andronikos IV* 84
    VIII *Manuel II, Paleologus* 87

THE SORCERER

The Sorcerer Contemplates His Beginnings 92
The Sorcerer in His Wrath 94

The Sorcerer's Prayer 96
The Sorcerer to His Long-Lost Love 98

PROPHECIES AND INTIMATIONS

Medieval Tale. 102
Bone Poem. 103
Nuclear Spring. 104
One Entropic Evening. 107
My Age 108
Song of the Minor Poets 110

Notes 113

To John Sevcik,
the first poet I ever looked up to
not merely because he was taller.

INTRODUCTION:
The Light at the End of the Tunnel

At the same time that it began replacing strict metre and rhyme with the egalitarian medium of prose, modern poetry supposedly got rid of the worst excesses and obscurities of the Victorian period—that is, before it replaced them in turn with its own obscurities, relative inaccessibility, and carefully contrived puzzles masquerading as profundity. Actually the Victorian period was one of tremendous accomplishment in all the major European languages, whether deployed in Europe or the Americas.

Of course, great modern poetry, whether by Ezra Pound, T.S. Eliot, E.E. Cummings, Cesare Vallejo, Pablo Neruda, or Lawrence Ferlinghetti, to cite just a few names at random, rises above all such restrictions and limitations. Certainly there are great poets alive today, even if not universally recognized, and all of them quite different one from the other. To cite just a few names at random again, there are Philip Lamantia, the great American Surrealist poet who lives in San Francisco; the no less remarkable, even if unclassifiable Marvin R. Hiemstra, who also lives in San Francisco; and the overly modest but just as remarkable Charlotte Barr of Hixson, Tennessee, formerly Sister Mary Anthony, the creator of a unique and all-inclusive kind of religious poetry that may be safely identified as Christian devotional and Mediterranean sensual.

But beyond these and other great figures of the Twentieth Century, there are many other excellent poets who do not aspire to greatness but only to express themselves in their own unique and appropriate ways—who seek primarily to entertain and to write out of their private lives. In this aspiration they succeed, and they do so with seriousness, conviction, honestly, and considerable skill. Darrell Schweitzer falls into this latter and very broad category, and is in fact an outstanding exponent of contemporary imaginative literature: among his many other accomplishments he has functioned as editor of the resuscitated magazine *Weird Tales* now for a number of years with both literary distinction and commercial success.

Darrell is a solid and excellent storyteller, and GROPING TOWARD THE LIGHT, with its generally objective tone and focus, as well as with its professionally honed narratives, forms a most refreshing exception to the most flagrant excesses of modern poetry. The subject matter here is horror, terror, and fantasy, no less than history taken with a large and beneficial dose of imagination, as well as with a delightfully wicked sense of humor. Here are fine medieval ballads or ballad-like poems, as for example, "Two Knights," which relates a poignant and especially touching exchange between a living father and a ghostly son. Here are also opulent historical characters and unique historical moments insightfully revealed. My own favorites deal with ancient Rome and medieval Constantinople: "Roman Coins," "Heraclius in Constantinople," Romulus Augustulus Deposed," and "Manuel II, Paleologus." However, Darrell is equally skilled in the poems dealing with horror, terror, and pure grue; or on the other hand in his too brief cycle concerning the archetypal sorcerer. The poet has mastered a fine and very flexible kind of syllabic line, part free verse, part blank verse, achieving many definitive and memorable passages that haunt the shared corridors of our collective imagination.

Particularly appealing is the final section of poems under the title *Prophecies and Intimations*, and the chief selection therein, the autobiographical opus "My Age," written as recently as December of 1999. This is Darrell's own personal meditation, at the age of 47, on his own mortality, and at one and the same time it is rueful, humorous, hopeful, and moving. The collection ends with a brief but very welcome section of informative, insightful, and witty notes, and as a Romanophile as fervent as Darrell himself, I can only wish that they went on at much greater length.

That this collection is the rewarding and individual book that it is, in truth, reflects considerable credit on Darrell Schweitzer. In a type of poetry that can generically be classified as fantasy and science fiction, or science fantasy—dominated as it undeniably has been at least in English during the Twentieth Century by such major figures as H.P. Lovecraft and Clark Ashton Smith among others—it would seem that Monsieur Schweitzer's poetry owes no great indebtedness to anyone but himself. That alone is a significant accomplishment, and it is a distinct pleasure to partake of the entertainment and enlightenment provided by GROPING TOWARD THE LIGHT.

Donald Sidney-Fryer,
the Last of the Courtly Poets,
Los Angeles, California,
7 February 2000, or if you will,
in accordance with the ancient
Roman system of dating, A.U.C. 2753

Apparitions
Faintly Seen

He Unwraps Himself

He unwraps himself, like a Christmas package,
the ribboned clothing, the greeting-card hair,
nose and ears, nipples, penis, cast aside,
off —

He unfolds himself, with silent grace;
the face is next, a delicate mask,
lifted away to reveal
the skull beneath the skin;

Stealing phrases from John Webster —
Or was it Marlowe? One of
those leotarded guys — he unlocks himself,
declaiming, "Come Sirrah! Gut me like a fish,
and give these groundlings
their sup of gore!"

Frenzied and fierce, he unbinds himself,
bloody sinews, lungs and heart,
the deeper flesh all steaming
at his feet, the gray-white skeleton
chattering in the dark, "But wait, my Love! There's more!"

At the very last, he reveals himself,
bones crinkled, heaped like newspaper,
the flickering candle's flame of his genuine self,
soul's truth, there, unadorned.
"Dearest, what you see is what you get."

But she hastily escapes through
shattered French windows,
and the night breeze
blows the candle out.

Each Evening
Emily Dreamed of the Grave

Each evening Emily dreamed of the grave,
voiceless and trapped in the stifling dark,
clinging to memories trickling away,
like sand in an hourglass, until she forgot
who she had been and whom she had loved,
tears and laughter, work and play,
bag and baggage of a life that is gone.

Even her name rattled away,
and this dream-corpse surrendered,
to a dream of her own:
the dawn's glaring light,
a stranger still asleep beside her,
and someone else's children in the hall,
shouting and clattering
on their way to breakfast.

All through the day,
amid chores, at meals,
pausing as she read a book,
or even as she made love,
she remembered her death,
and the touch of the grave.

"This must be resolved," her therapist told her.
"Wake up! Does the Chinese sage dream he has wings,
or does the butterfly dream it is a philosopher?
Wake up and see!"

And skeletal fingers shattered the coffin wood,
to claw their way upward through soft, muddy earth.

The Skeptics

Think of it as the plot
of a lost Greek comedy:
Gorgias, the stern philosopher,
doesn't believe in the gods.
and has raised his son, Philemon,
to doubt all things, save only
the head, heart, and hands of Man.

But on his deathbed,
the old fellow gets religion,
while downstage the boy rages
that his dad's a sell-out,
a coward, hypocrite, and fool.

Then the gods appear,
invisible to Philemon,
but so numerous that they crowd the stage,

dazzling in their gaudy costumes,
whispering incomprehensibly among themselves
as Hades bears Gorgias off.

In the epilogue,
the philosopher's ghost tries to explain,
that he hasn't been inconsistent.
He merely extended his doubt to include
the head, heart, and hands of Man,
which always fail in the end.

But Philemon can hear none of this,
raised as he was
to disbelieve in ghosts.

I Know That I Have
Slept Among the Dead

I know that I have slept among the dead,
resting in the comfortable darkness of the tombs
of the wealthy, storied, and beloved,
whose names I've quite forgotten.

I am certain, too, that once I felt
the earth's firm touch upon my bones,
soothing and reasonless, of infinite depth,
a blanket to smother all of my pain.

I remember distinctly the sound of the wind
howling for just a little while,
and the water dripping for a time,
and my own dust trickling down, briefly.

But somehow the infestation of flesh returned,
and the torturer's metaphysical fire
has jolted my brain, popped my eyes open,
leaving me to protest once again
the outrage of resurrection.

I Want to Be a Vampire

"I want to be a vampire,"
the little girl said.
She was even more a child to my eyes
with her black lipstick, eye-shadow,
leather, metal, and powdered-on pallor,
her knee-high boots and affectations of despair.

One of the damned, she would have me believe,
a friendless night-wanderer ripping out throats
of those she once loved;
a little girl playing a little girl's game.

And yet I have to admit
that it was her pain that attracted me to her,
and that her emptiness
was the secret of her appeal.

What If the Dead Are Laughing?

What if the dead are laughing,
huddled in their coffins like Zen monks in their cells,
comprehending at last the infinitely reverberating joke
that is the universe?

What if the dead are laughing *at me*,
locked in rictus hilarity as they contemplate
my most intimate desires,
delusions, and peccadilloes?

No, what I'm really afraid of
is that their laughter is as mindless as the wind,
a mere echo groping in the dark
toward some unremembered punchline.

What if the dead are laughing?

I am the Ghost

I am the ghost of the final hour.
It's my footsteps you hear in the empty hall,
when the feast is over and all the guests are gone.
Among the echoing, expected shadows,
in the beloved old house,
now abandoned and stripped bare,
I remember.

I am the ghost of those little hurts,
you said were nothing at all,
the ghost of words you should have said and words you
never did,
and of names without faces,
just on the tip of your tongue.
whispering on the back stair,
I remain.

I am the ghost of little fires,

not of burning cities or the fall of empires;

I lack the quality of apocalypse.

Though I can make an emperor tremble in a dream,

or a madman burn in his mind.

Nothing fades.

I am the ghost of a hundred thousand names:

called Nagging Doubt, I Should Have Done,

and It's Too Late,

dripping, chain-rattling *deja vu.*

At the inevitable, cliched funeral in the rain,

I shuffle behind you all the way to the lip of the grave

and bounce back jauntily, grinning.

Heretical Gospel

Lazarus, resurrected,
locked in his shuttered room,
still stinks of the grave,
and knows to his bones
that nothing can render him clean.

For Lazarus, resurrected,
dreams of that soundless void
from which he was hauled,
like a fish on a hook,
into the thundering sunlight.

Now Lazarus, resurrected,
spends the whole of his time,
in rapturous conversation,
with silent and unseen companions,
speaking the speech of the dead.

Two Knights

The old knight rode through wood and waste,
    before first light of day.
The young knight met him on a hill
    above the darkened bay.

The old knight spoke; his armor gleamed
    beneath the brilliant stars.
"Come ride with me, brave sir," he said,
    "and celebrate the wars —

"Crusades for Christ, my son has fought,
    throughout the pagan lands,
and relics of the Cross he's won,
    and held in trembling hands.

"A mighty ship, with banners bright,
    this morn on yonder shore
shall rest, and so my son comes home,
    to wander nevermore."

Then came they to the wooden bridge,
    where living water flowed.
The old knight clattered straight across;
    the young drew rein and slowed.

"Come ride with me," the old knight said
    "to welcome home my son.
Come praise his name; come praise his fame;
    come praise the deeds he's done."

The young knight sat in silence there
    in darkness on the hill.
His voice was like a cold, faint breeze,
    quiet, rustling, still.

"I am the ghost of your dear son,
    in bloody battle slain.
I cannot cross the living stream,
    nor ride with you again.

"My coffin lies within the ship
    that anchors on the morrow.
Father, greet me there alone,
    in silence and in sorrow.

"And speak not of my battles won,
    my glory, or my worth,
for all the dead are equal when
    they lie beneath the earth.

"The rogue, the slave, the king, the lord,
    the wicked and the just —
What matter names or words or deeds,
    when all are clay and dust?"

The old knight rode to meet the ship,
    in silence and in sorrow.
He laid his son within a grave,
    and died upon the morrow.

Invocation

Mother Hecate! Mistress of Night!
Goddess of dread, of pain and of fright,
Goddess of graves, of death's holy fire,
Goddess of daggers, of hate and desire!

Come to the hanged man, who turns in the air.
Come as a wolf, as a hound, as a mare.
Come to the crossroads, with torch and with sword.
Come, as we call thee, come at our word!

We who would serve thee, offer up blood,
of black lamb and black dog, and infant new-born.
We who would love thee, offer our souls,
to murder and witchcraft, secretly sworn.

Goddess of darkness, bringer of woes!
Go from us after our covenant's made.

Make those who hunt us with good cause afraid—

Goddess of vengeance, visit our foes!

After the Night

Dusk ship
wooden ship.
Night ship
stone ship.
Dawn ship
dust ship.

In the whispering dark time they came for me, in the
night; and they bore me gently down to the mirror-smooth sea;
where their tiny hands tore away the spider web veil of my flesh;
and I lay exposed.

And they began their work, so quietly, so gingerly:

From my bones they formed the frame
of a mighty vessel, binding it
together with my ligaments.

My arms made fine spars, my ribs the curving hull,

both legs together, a sturdy mast,

my folded hands set in the bow to part the waters.

They had preserved my skin, tanned it; stretched it over
the whole body, sealed against leaks.

They hung my face upon the mast, a sacrifice to the winds.

Then I was launched from the bloody sand,

into the smooth, black, tideless silence,

my lidless eyes ever searching for the blessed shore

of the land ruled by two brothers, Sleep and Death.

And ever the black sun sets;

the white moon rises.

My scream is unheard.

I am called Argo.

Let Me Glide Gently
Into My Death

"Let me glide gently into my death.
Float my barge swiftly away from the sun.
Carry me solemnly up the far bank.
Leave me to listen to immortal song."

Thus were the words of the murdered queen,
when she felt the poison course her veins,
and knew her last intrigue had failed.

"Let me glide gently into my death,
out of the reach of the rebel's revenge.
All that I've done was only to serve
that higher conscience of scepter and state."

So spake the restless tyrant king,
alone in his tent, at battle's dawn,
pacing to keep off the terror of dreams.

"Let me glide gently into my death.
This holy hunger gnaws at my bones!
Just one little coin to rattle my cup,
then roll this old carcass into a ditch!"

Such were the words the beggar cried,
sputtering through his rotten teeth,
as he plucked at the robes of wedding guests.

All three died within an hour
and came as one before the gods,
to be weighed and noted, measured out.

But found they nowhere loving gods,
nor gods who yield to human pleas.
These were gods of *Do it now*,
I have spoken, It is writ,
implacable, thundering, slightly bored,
the gods of easy answers.
The beggar was given a coin for his cup,
and sent to silence in the dark.

The queen was left to howl and haunt,
and weep hot blood in ancient halls.
The king was hanged upon a tree
until the birds that pecked his eyes
built their nest in his golden crown.

These three came before the gods,
gliding gently into death!

Still There

You're still there.
The first time I saw you outside my window,
I thought it was a dream.
That would make sense:
Your dark eyes inscrutable as always,
cheeks and forehead aglow like candle wax
with some inner fire,
surely no mere trick of glass
and reflected streetlights.
Yes, a dream, in which you wept
and demanded, "Do you love me?"
But I didn't hear your voice,
and the only sound was from the traffic.

Do I? Still?
Dearest Heart, if I couldn't say so even then,
before all that went between us,

all that happened,

all that ended,

how can you expect an answer now?

Cherish the mystery; it's all we have.

And yet you're still there every night,

and it is not a dream:

You, in the darkness,

swaying in the breeze like a paper lantern,

hovering like some preposterous moth,

inches beyond my window pane,

fifteen storeys up.

The House-Guest's Ghost Story

In the end it came to this:

The phantom thing
had stood without my chamber door,
scratching and muttering,
—No! it was not the wind!—
moaning for entirely too long,
and I, unable to bear the terror of it,
flung wide the door to confront
the dreadful apparition.

But I only saw myself,
as if I stood before a mirror.

And, unable to bear the terror of it,
the figure before me fled.

And I entered through the open door
and searched the empty chamber.
There was no other door.
The windows were locked.
I even looked under the bed.

Therefore I've walked these halls
for three hundred years now,
continuing my desperate search,
uncertain that I shall be able to bear
the terror of its conclusion.

The Man in the Wind

The Man in the Wind came riding swiftly toward me.
The Man in the Wind came racing to my call.
I plucked a root; I burned a stone; I wrapped a penny in a leaf;
I raised my arms and cried aloud,
and the Man in the Wind was there.

I think he rode a thin gray horse
of vapor and of ash;
I think he wore a tall, peaked hat,
a cloak like a wind-filled sail;
but the night was dark; I could not see—
Did he scowl or did he laugh?

I made to speak; he raised his hand;
the moonlight glistened on his bones.
And *silence*, and the air was still;
his voice like a rustling reed:

"Ask me not where your love has gone.

I know but shall not tell.

Seek not to know how long you'll live;

nor if you'll go to Hell;

nor where in the earth the treasures lie,

where ships are sunk, when war begins,

nor the names of the peaks where the witches fly,

for hideous, secret sins.

I've watched your kind since the Garden gate;

I filled the Argo's sails.

I saw brave Hector meet his fate,

and Helen's beauty fail.

Don't strive too much, but live each day,

as fully as you can.

Feel grief and joy while yet you may,

and measure not your span.

"Over-reacher—

You cut a stone; you drag a stone;

you raise it into place:

a pharaoh's tomb, a house of God,

a castle built for war.
If truly you must do a thing,
if truly you must know a thing,
then drag your stone, then raise it up;
mix mortar with your blood.
Then strive, strive, strive,
my foolish, would-be Faustus.
No spirit can give you an easy answer."

He turned his back and galloped swiftly from me.
The trees bent low as the Man in the Wind sped by.
I stood aghast; my mind was blank;
his answer numbed my soul.
The fire gone out, forgotten was
the question I'd meant to ask him.

Old Father Stone,

(an enigmatic myth with wandering rhyme)

With hatred and with thunder,
the grinding of his teeth,
the vengeful giant wakens,
buried far beneath.

Granite Father, Sire Stone,
devours all his sons:
the wicked one, the doleful one,
the child all alone.

Fearful Father Vengeance,
his stone lips red with gore,
cries out in surprising grief
and turns, and turns some more

to places where his children played,
toward their mother's grave.
Bloody, empty-handed,
He cannot hope to save

his kingdom or his crown,
his scepter, tumbling down.

Silent, in defeat,
he lies beneath our feet,

and won't let us forget

his sorrows or his joys,
how he gobbled little boys
and countless hosts of men.

The Wizard's Glass

Do not gaze in the wizard's glass.
You'll only see yourself there.
That mere reflection makes you ask,
how it somehow might have been
if you had walked another path,
or had not married so-and-so,
or killed the fool who needed death,
or simply wiped the planet clean.

That mere reflection makes you ask,
if your thoughts are wise and vast,
or or sad delusions, puddle-deep,
and whether words can sing.
And does a living lump of clay,
differ from common dirt?
And is all friendship, joy, or love,
but glittering gold for fools?

And is the one reflected there,
in the darkness of the glass,
benumbed, bereft of joy and pain,
still a living man at all,
or but cold shadow, unnamed Void,
child of Nothing, sire to No One?

The demon in the wizard's glass
dwells too in every heart.
So do not gaze into that glass,
and shun the wizard's art.

Mad Song the First

When, at last, death would be the greatest gift,
I shall withhold this boon from you.
I know you'd do the same for me,
for isn't love a kind of hatred,
and hatred a kind of love?

Abomination, that's what you called me.
You said that I could never love,
any more than Jack the Ripper did.

But, my dear, Saucy Jack cherished his girls,
so thoroughly,
painstakingly,
intimately
did he explore them,
particularly that last one, Mary Kelly.

Do you see yon dark, dark road,
that wanders through the broad daylight?

And do you see yon bright, bright road,
expiring in the dark of night?

Both are the roads to Hell, my dear,
where you and I this hour must go.

Not Your Typical
Horror Poem

If this were your typical horror poem,
I'd have ripped your eyes out in the first two lines,
peeling back the skin of your cheeks,
so your grimacing redmask can sing along
while I play on your slippery bones
like some lunatic one-man band,
the new-slit mouth beneath your chin yammering,
as we two dance in mad embrace
all the way to Hell.

But this is not a typical horror poem,
so I'm not going to do those things to you.

At least not right away.

It Wasn't Haunted

Returning,
I asked to see my old room,
and the landlord, dubious,
led me up the creaking stairs I'd last climbed
half a lifetime ago,
unlocked the door and swung it wide.

The room was just a room.
Sunlight streamed in through the dusty windows.
The walls continued upright,
the floorboards met neatly, sensibly, firm.
I ducked beneath the sloping ceiling,
and got paint chips in my hair.

I could still see the marks where my bed once was,
where I'd slept so many nights,
dreaming a young man's furious dreams,

or lay awake, listening,
as my life was hammered out and shaped
upon the anvil of time.

True evil can be born in such a place,
or prophetic dreams may come,
yet afterward there's only the room:
windows, ceiling, floor, and dust,
but no ghosts, because we carry them all away
within us when we leave.

Death's Favorite Snapshot

The perfect horror found in nature:
a praying mantis poised on a milkweed,
claws at ready,
while out of reach of those claws
a yellow-jacket wasp devours the mantis,
starting at the nether end,
wriggling into the growing cavity
where the abdomen used to be.

And still the mantis stupidly waits,
for a dinner it can no longer digest.
"Look at it this way," says the wasp.
"The pain may be unbearable,
but at least you get to wear
my splendid, striped coat."

History
and
Other Enigmas

Concerning the Fate of
Philip, Emissary of Pope Alexander III
to Prester John

This much might well be true,

that the pope wrote a letter,

dated September 22, 1177,

and entrusted his physician, Philip,

to deliver it, commanding him

to seek out the fabled domain

of John, Priest, Lord of the Four Indias,

most puissant Christian monarch of Asia,

and secure an alliance against the Saracens.

Philip never returned.

It is easy enough to imagine

that loyal and learned man

butchered by bandits,

or rotting in a dungeon far away,

or dying obscurely in some God-forsaken village

while strangers shook their heads sadly,

unable to comprehend a single word of his delirium,

and then placed the letter, unopened,

at the feet of a barbarous stone idol

until wind and rain and mice did the rest.

Or maybe the wastelands just swallowed him up.

No, I say.

We must demand more than that.

Let us insist, at least,

that brave Philip reached the wild marches of Asia,

encountering whole wandering herds

of seven-horned bulls,

and lions of red, green, black, and blue,

and griffins, which carry off oxen,

and Yllerion, which have wings like razors,

and, of course, unicorns.

Let us say, too,

that he crossed the Sea of Sand,

as Alexander did, carried aloft
by one of those griffins,
and came at last
to the river of precious stones,
and the land of shadow,
and the country of headless men,
whose eyes grow beneath their shoulders,
and other such marvels as are described
by numerous excellent authors.

I am certain that he beheld the Phoenix,
dying, burning, resurrected,
and I think that he secured a drop
of that holy oil
which bleeds from a dry tree,
a mere day's journey from the Earthly Paradise.

And I have dreamed that Philip was received kindly
at the court of Prester John,
and allowed to rest,
while the pope's letter was read.

46

What then? He did not return.

Prester John's answer remains a mystery.

There *are* mysteries, after all.

I merely insist on certain standards

so the trackless waste

won't swallow us all.

The Truth About Caspar Hauser

(1812-1833)

1

Now, only the facts remain:
Caspar Hauser, reputed child of goblins,
raised from his earliest years
in some lightless, undocumented dungeon,
ignorant of his jailer's name,
hardly able to speak at all,
or even walk;
this unlikely exile appeared
on the street of a respectable German village,
a mere, shabby enigma,
until he became the fad of Europe
for a blinding instant of unbearable fame.
Then Caspar Hauser bled his life away,
stabbed in the snow,

no footprints anywhere but his own,
one final confusion in the ill-rehearsed prologue
to a play canceled on opening night.

2

I think Caspar Hauser had all the answers.
Complete unto himself in his buried prison,
graduate with honors
from the University of Indeterminate Pain,
degree in hand,
he wandered forth,
took one look at the squalid, brawling, human world,
and, selfish, wicked, and wise boy that he was,
hardened his heart,
and bore his treasure back
into the mystery
whence he came.

The Lost Dauphins

In life, of course, Louis XVI had only one son,
but after his head was off, how the family grew and grew,
like toads, generated spontaneously
out of the puddle of royal gore.

First there came Hervagault (Jean Marie), son of a tailor,
then Persat, the old sailor,
and Fontolive, bricklayer,
the Three Stooges of the Terror,
who might have achieved low comedy,
but for their swift and messy deaths.

Mathurin Brunneau,
common criminal,
caught the torch when it fell to him,
and maybe even hoped, for a brief time,
to convince people that he was king of France.

Such were his fifteen minutes of fame,
a century and a half before Warhol.

It was Henri Herbert who first attempted
to raise these impostures to the level of art,
adding a suitable dash of pathos,
fairy-tale, romance, and even sublime myth:
the dying child substituted for the real prince,
who is then smuggled to safety inside a wooden horse,
raised to manhood in a remote, craggy castle,
seeking his destiny
in Egypt, among the Mameluks,
up the Amazon, with wise, knowing savages,
amid the ruins of lost cities,
protected by an emperor,
visited by an angel
(in improbable tall hat and long coat)
who warned him of danger,
told him to keep the Sabbath,
and vanished—
quite a fellow,

this Indiana Jones de Bourbon von Munchausen!
At least he was entertaining.
Bold Henri never got his crown,
but he published his memoirs,
and spent his old age crabbedly, ceaselessly,
trying to rewrite the ending,
while waiting for Hollywood to call.

The Pole, Naundorf, was but a grubby shadow,
too old for the part,
convicted incendiary,
all-around loser,
disappointment.
(Died 1845.)

And, at last, Monty Python's Life of Louis,
another mock-epic,
with a kinder, gentler ending,
the true story of Eleazar,
the half-breed Iroquois mental defective,
who hit his head on a rock at age thirteen,

and suddenly everything was clear:

He remembered sitting in the lap of a beautiful lady

who might have been Marie Antoinette.

(Or maybe not.)

He recoiled from a picture of Simon,

the lost prince's vile gaoler.

He even *looked* like a Bourbon,

and left people scratching their heads and musing,

"Well, you don't suppose?"

His very befuddlement was beguiling,

for once that terrific moment of revelation was past,

poor Eleazar was never quite sure.

"If I am not mistaken," he said as he signed the document

abdicating in favor of Louis Philippe.

The French government gave Eleazar a pension.

He married, found other things to do,

and lived out his life,

transformed in an instant,

as if touched by Henri Herbert's angel.

His mind healed; he never got to be a king,
but he became a whole man.

And what of the truth?
Ah yes, that.
Imagine merely that the tortured child
vanished from his cell in 1795,
inexplicably,
into the darkness,
to dance with Anastasia.

Another Enigma

One night, in his despair,
the Man in the Iron Mask scratched some words
onto a silver dinner plate,
and hurled it from his window.
He watched the plate
soaring like a flying saucer in the moonlight,
over fields forever beyond his reach.

A peasant found the plate and brought it back,
hoping for a reward.
"Do you know what this says?" the jailer demanded.
"Alas, sir, I cannot read."
"Then your ignorance has saved you. Go!"
And the peasant went, with his life,
clutching a small coin, now part
of a legend he could never understand.

In truth, the jailer didn't understand it either,

because the message on the plate

was written in no language yet seen on Earth,

and may be only roughly translated:

"I am:

Philippe, twin brother of the King of France,

or the King himself,

or the bastard son of a duke,

or some other indiscretion of the nobility,

or a time-traveler from the future,

or a figment of my own imagination,

or a ghost.

Choose one and only one.

Please."

Even years after the plate had been returned to him,

the prisoner never checked one off,

because by then

the Man in the Iron Mask

no longer knew the answer.

The Shipwreck

(from the imaginary Anglo-Saxon)

The stranger spoke, unlocked his word-hoard:

I sailed from a fair land, far to the west,
where bright fields bloom, where sun seldom sets,
a wondrous land; I have lost that land,
lost too my lord, my ring-giving lord,
gracious and good, guided by God.
Now cut off from kinsmen, warriors and wives,
I wander with new folk, who know not my name.
Hear then:

Aella I am, Aethelwulf's son.
My strong-hulled ship was called *Whale Friend*.
Stricken by storm, wearied by wind,
shorn of her shields by the sharp sea-teeth,
Whale Friend foundered.

Friends found their fates in furious foam,
comrades all drowned, cast to their doom.
Seized I the mast, snapped by waves' might,
borne by wild waters, for days without end,
surviving the sun, the searing of thirst,
cast on this shore.

Two years and ten have I dwelt in these dales.
The men of this country are Christian and kind;
they've fed me and clothed me;
they've kept me from harm.
They call me Old Father and Wanderer Far.
Within Christ's house they sing mass for my soul.
Yet still I long for the sea, long for my home.

Never on earth shall a man find true peace.

The Outcast

(from the imaginary Anglo-Saxon)

Let us hear now of the heroes of old,
of Constantine, the Christian king,
and Arthur, dread wielder of the wonder-sword.

Their flesh is dust; their bones are cold;
their ghosts are gathered on the fens.

Let us tell the tales of brave warriors,
of Hnaef, who held the hall,
and Aelfric, master of the sea-steeds.

Their flesh is dust; their bones are cold;
their ghosts are gathered on the fens.

Let us sing of poets, recall the songs,
of Caedmon, who wrought the words of man's beginning,

and Eothere, who warned the world of future woe.
Their flesh is dust; their bones are cold;
their ghosts are gathered on the fens.

My lord lies slain; his stead is burnt;
his thanes are fallen on the field;
my people cast into the dark earth-cave.

Their flesh is dust; their bones are cold;
their ghosts are gathered on the fens.

Alone have I lived, to wend the ways of weary exile.
I sing of the past, while foreign lords rule the land.
There is no one to listen, none who knew the days that were.

Their flesh is dust; their bones are cold;
their ghosts are gathered on the fens.

I know this: that all men shall die,
their lives shorn short, their deeds soon done;

soon lords and folk shall sink into sleep;

soon great shall be gone; soon lowly lost;

soon shall my foemen fall before years.

Soon shall I be with my lord.

Roman Coins

They're all here, the murdered men:
Gallienus, looking alternatively heroic and prissy,
as he really was,
with fabulous beasts on his reverses,
merely because they caught his fancy,
before the assassins came.
Marcus Aurelius Probus, stern-jawed and brave,
entered among the gods.
Aurelian, who restored the world,
and dropped it in a careless moment.

And a gallery of the wicked:
Puffy-faced Nero, his uneasy gaze
on the lookout for the inevitable Furies
with their fiery whips.
Elagabalus, cherubic boy,
whose pranks astounded even

the exquisites of a degenerate age.

Here's Romulus and Remus, on Caracalla's reverse—
intriguing selection for a fratricide.

Political mayflies, ephemeral jokes:
Maxentius: TO THE ETERNITY OF THE EMPEROR.
Drowned in the Tiber swiftly enough.
Valens: THE GLORY OF THE ROMANS.
Shown dragging a barbarian by the hair,
this pompous, antique Custer,
whom the Goths dragged by the short hairs
in several directions at once,
when he lost at Adrianople.

Apostate Julian,
Homeric, proud, and very stiff,
posing in his theatrical beard,
like a kid in a high school yearbook,
his eyes toward Olympus,
where the gods are already dead.

And Imperator Darrell Schweitzer,
Pius, Felix, Pontifex Max.
Laurel leaves or radiate crown?
Was he ever deified?
Scrape off the dirt of two thousand years
and maybe we'll see if
hyper-inflation rendered him base,
or under the patina there's anything at all.

I'd rather not decipher
this message from my intimate past.
The archaeology of the present is quite enough
for ancient autobiography.

Signs and Portents

(dinner conversation, Rome, A.D. 394)

"The word has come from Egypt
that the Apis Bull has appeared again,
garlanded in all its expected magnificence,
and that a voice thunders from the Serapeum,
unintelligible, but comforting nonetheless,
in its thoroughly traditional frightfulness.
There's even talk of the Phoenix,
and of a new age, beginning,
or a golden age, returning.
The Egyptian skies are filled with portents."

"The word has come from Aquilea,
that the truth-loving emperor Theodosius
has utterly crushed the upstart Eugenius,
and the murderer Arbogastes,
and all their heathen cronies.

There were the armies of Christ and Jupiter
objectively weighed in the balance,
and at the crucial moment a miraculous wind
hurled the spears of the pagans
back into their faces.
The only voices that day crying,
were of the wicked, swiftly dying.
At Aquilea, the skies are filled with angels."

"How very fortunate, then,
that you and I
aren't the sort to give credence
to preposterous rumors,
or to idle, wagging tongues."

Romulus Augustulus Deposed

(4 September, A.D. 476)

Thus perished the empire of the Romans,
in the reign of such-and-such (depending on how you count)
successor to Augustus.

That's how Jordanes reported it,
as an apocalypse.
What did he know,
a terminally depressed Goth
a hundred years later?
He lacked perspective.

Did anyone actually notice the end when it came?
In Rome itself, that summer,
the price of grain remained about the same.
Blue-gray dust stirred in the empty Forum.

Idlers chatted in the shade of the temple porches,
something about another coup, up north.

In Ravenna the Little Augustus surely noticed.
He wore a purple robe for a while.
Then rough men came and took it away,
and told him that his father,
the Patrician Orestes, was dead.
Romulus was old enough to understand.
He must have passed some fear-filled nights,
before he learned that he was being sent away
on a comfortable pension to live in Campania,
not merely a has-been at sixteen but a never-was.
What life he found there, what longings and loves,
what remembrances, we simply do not know.
Perhaps he wept for his father.

So why did anyone mark the epoch?
It's because of the dust in the Forum,
which was the shade of an ancient Lady,
with crested helmet, spear, and burnished shield,

the ghost of the goddess Roma,

rising unnoticed on the afternoon breeze,

to summon first, Justinian,

and then so many others.

BYZANTINE PORTRAITS

I

Heraclius in Constantinople

(A.D. 622)

On that night when it truly seemed

that Christ had died in vain,

and all the work of his apostles was soon to perish,

the emperor stood on the city walls and beheld,

across the straits, along the Asian shore,

the glow of burning churches, as far as the eye could see.

Behind him, Avar campfires circled the capital

like numberless, evil stars.

He waited.

In the morning, nothing had changed.

The fires still smudged the sky.

Yet he found the sign he sought,

no flaming, celestial vision such as Constantine had enjoyed,

but merely this:

in the face of each young soldier, looking up at him,

in the eyes of old women, in the cries of children,

in the mutterings of courtiers,

in the secret whisper behind their words,

he found the explicit belief,

that he, Basileus of the Romans, God's regent on Earth,

possessed the authority to work a miracle,

and heal the bleeding world.

No less was expected of him.

Though the barbarians were still outside the walls,

and the churches of Asia burned,

and the Holy Wood, stained with the Savior's blood,

languished in Ctesiphon amid the mocking pagans,

Heraclius found hope,

and humbly,

thanking God and repenting his sins,

he set forth to equal

the glories of Alexander.

II

Heraclius in Persia

(A.D. 623)

Of course we slaughtered the defenders,
for they had defiled with unclean hands
the city of our Savior's death,
and carried off that sacred Wood
on which the Lord God bled.

We took Ganzaca,
near to ancient Nineveh,
and waded through Persian corpses,
their blood splashing about our ankles,
when someone said, "Augustus, you have to see this."

I followed, and there in the great hall
stood the sky-reaching idol of the monster Khusru,
King of Kings,
who had shed the blood of a hundred thousand Romans.

The abomination stood
in the center of a carven marble universe,
the winged sun and planets bowed down
in abject adoration.

Every man who beheld this awful thing,
drew his breath in astonishment,
and couldn't let it out.
Time stopped.

I gave orders at once that the image should be destroyed,
smashed with hammers, then ground into powder
and mixed with wine like the Golden Calf,
a measure saved in a flask for Khusru to drink
when we finally caught up with him.
Yet no soldier could be made to raise his hand against it,
and the spectators had to be dragged off
blindfolded, until they recovered their senses.

I alone had the strength to turn away of my own will,
seared as I was with blazing hope,

for the marble king did not hold in his lifeless fingers,

or number among his playthings,

the True Cross of Christ.

It must still be ahead of us somewhere,

waiting to be rescued.

Therefore I rallied the men,

and they destroyed the shrine with great zeal,

and we continued on our way.

III

Heraclius in Jerusalem

(A.D. 637)

He came like a thief and left like a fugitive,
unwilling to tarry more than a single night,
he who had retrieved out of defiling pagan hands
the priceless Wood on which the Savior bled.
He dared not lose it again,
he who had crushed the mighty Persian
and now fled powerless before Mahomet's armies,
as if before a great wind.
The True Cross reached Constantinople safely,
but the emperor,
in the last throes of degrading disease,
feared to cross the straits
until a pontoon bridge was built, lined with trees,
feigning a country road.
In his despair, Heraclius may well have cried out,
a touch blasphemously,

"My God, my God, why have you forsaken me?"

But in his heart of hearts, he knew.

It was because of his sin, of course,

because of "the accursed thing."

IV

Justinian the Second Rages

(A.D. 705)

He actually came back.

Deposed emperors aren't supposed to do that.

But there's more:

A storm caught him at sea,

and when it seemed certain that he and all his companions

would soon perish,

a toady, of the patented sort even wandering exiles retain,

a cringing, blubbering creature, suggested

that maybe Lord Justinian ought to forgive his enemies,

humble himself before God, and promise to build a few churches.

That sort of expedient had worked under similar

circumstances in the past.

(Galla Placidia did it in 423.)

"I will *not* forgive my enemies!" was the reply.

"If I ever get out of this,

I'll hunt down and kill every last one of them!

Do you hear me?

Do you hear me?"

(It was uncertain who was being addressed.)

Justinian shouted down the thunder.

The storm stopped. The waters grew calm,

and, in the company of some nasty-tempered Bulgars,

he landed at Constantinople,

climbed in through a sewer,

and once more ascended

the throne of his ancestors.

They called him "Slit-Nose,"

for, so mutilated, he had been sent away the first time,

on the naive belief that a physically imperfect man

could never be Basileus.

Justinian knew better.

He butchered his would-be successors.

The streets ran with blood.

Widows cried to heaven.

Dungeons were filled with doomed men who cried out
whatever their torturers wanted them to.
That had worked under similar circumstances in the past.
(Caligula, Nero, Domitian, Commodus.)

But Justinian inevitably went too far
— and they did far more than slit his nose again—
when he sent a fleet to raze Cherson, the place of his exile,
massacre the citizenry, sow the ground with salt, etc.
as had perhaps worked under (not quite) similar
circumstances in the past (*Carthago delenda est.*),
but not now.

For Justinian had forgotten
that thunder only lasts for a short time,
and a storm soon passes.

V

Theodosius the Third

(A.D. 717)

Theodosius the Third
has no qualifications whatsoever to rule.
He's just a tax clerk,
with an unfortunate,
imperial-sounding name.

Therefore rebellious armies swept him up,
like a leaf in a raging torrent,
and if he cried out in protest or in terror,
no one heard his voice,
as the multitudes acclaimed
the perpetual and ever-victorious Augustus,
Theodosius, under God,
Basileus of the Romans.

He can only sit in silence
in the great palace in Constantinople,

motionless in his gold-brocaded robes,

beneath his heavy crown,

like one of the holy icons

soon to be outlawed

by the swift-approaching Leo.

VI

Michael VIII (1261-1282)

They say that he was so amazingly wicked,

that when he died

his coffin floated in the air

because the earth would not accept him,

just like Mahound.

But this was the restorer of New Rome!

True, he stepped to the throne over the corpse of a child,

but he drove the horrible Latins out of the capital,

and cleansed the holy altar of Hagia Sophia,

where once a harlot sat.

He reigned as an emperor should,

confounding his enemies,

and if certain measures were necessary,

they were necessary.

Surely God will understand.

Thanks to Michael,

the memorious, imperial dream continued,

stirring echoes amid the roofless houses,

parading shadows in the empty streets,

for another two centuries.

That must count for something.

VII

Andronikos IV

(1376-79)

The story is so incredible, it must be true:
Prince Andronikos, son of John the Unfortunate,
and Saudji, son of Sultan Murad,
found they that they envied and hated
their respective fathers,
this common treason providing
the basis for a short-lived friendship
as their conspiracy proceeded
and ended the way such things usually do.

And the Sultan decreed,
like Allah thundering from the mountain,
that Saudji should be blinded—
and he was, and he died—
and that, further, Basileus John
should burn out the eyes of his own son,
and his infant grandson too,

son of Andronikos, also called John.
And who could resist the mighty Sultan?

This is were the incredible part begins:
Andronikos recovered his sight
(or wasn't really blinded)
and somehow never lost his father's love,
and was entirely unworthy of it.
They say he strangled a black serpent in his prison,
a symbol of his own nature,
but that is a lie,
because his nature did not change.

Andronikos actually got out,
and reigned for three years,
until the Turk flicked him from his perch;
but even then Andronikos survived
and inspired the boy John to imitate him,
lock up grandpa once again,
and put on the storied crown,
of Constantine and Justinian the Great,

to the vast amusement of Murad,

who must have seen them all

as insects skittering around

inside a gold-plated eggshell

which has visibly begun to crack.

Manuel II, Paleologus

(1391-1423)

Manuel II, Paleologus,
true guardian of the ancient Roman name
in an age when nobody else cares,
a relic of the old and dying world,
is a small, dark man
with vast beard gone prematurely white,
so that he looks like some biblical patriarch
in a faded icon.

Manuel II, Paleologus
Caesar, Augustus, Basileus—
his capital is a hollow shell,
whole districts populated by echoes
or reverted to ploughed fields within the walls,
his imperial domain extending
no more than a day's ride beyond the city.

Manuel II, Paleologus
thought he had seen the end,
when Bayazid, called the Thunderbolt,
appeared before the gates
glowering amid his horde
and swearing the death
of every Christian who defied him.

Manuel prayed for a miracle,
and got one,
when the Mongol horde
scattered the Turks
like so many frightened blackbirds.

But Manuel II, Paleologus
was unable to recover any of the lost provinces
and had to be content repairing his walls,
for even God's regent on Earth is only allowed
just so many miracles.

Now he prays for a small mercy,

meaningless against the grand scale of eternity,

or even history,

and therefore easily granted:

that he might pass on what little remains to his sons,

and not be the last Basileus of the Romans.

Please God, not the last.

Not the last.

The Sorcerer

The Sorcerer
Contemplates His Beginnings

To think that once I was a child such as these,
a tumble of rags and dust in a village street,
or a trembling boy barely into his teens,
his heart thumping as he runs to meet
some sweetheart in the evening air.
The boy did not fear the darkness then,
nor ponder the mysteries of the Worm,
nor speak with thunder among the hills.
When did the fire begin to burn?

When he listened to whispers in the night,
and learned that death is but a door;
when demons raised him to some height,
promising kingdoms, gold, and more;
when first he walked a shadowed path,
quite unknown to most mankind,

seduced by sigils of the heart,
and inscrutable hieroglyphs of the mind.

Then the fire began to burn,
and sorcery sparked to life within.

The Sorcerer in His Wrath

1

Now is the time for the breaking of graves,
for the hour of vengeance has come 'round at last.
Now shall the dead lie embracing the living—
Let their foul kisses bring sharp screams of love!

I stand here in darkness while tall cities tumble,
while gold-draped corpses usurp the world's thrones.
I speak words of fire, of tempest, of earthquake:
My orison horror, and death my Amen.

2

Yet would I ask in a quieter voice,
what fool is this man who would thunder the skies?
What arrogant ass who thinks that his rage,

should speed on its way the mere passage of years?

This surely is Time's work: the ravening scythe,

the merciless glass, the withering touch.

When this one like all men is pitiful dust,

what matter his anger, his vengeance, his name?

The Sorcerer's Prayer

What if

dwelling among corpses but not actually dead,

I complete my centuried journey,

up to my thighs in unsensory dust,

and arrive at last before Death's throne

only to find it empty?

What if, then,

I usurp the Dread Lord's seat

and pass my judgment upon the worlds,

consigning to oblivion all human vanities,

but those vanities, vain and stubborn as they are,

refuse to go,

and kings still on their own thrones still thunder,

and lovers sigh,

and poets continue to scribble lines like these,

until my Sign of Doom

is but the shadow of my hand,
and my voice is just the wind?

I ask only
for a dialogue with the darkness,
until all my restless questions are finally answered
by encyclopedic silence,
and I come to master the sacred and secret lore
of nothing, absolutely.

The Sorcerer to His Long-Lost Love

Come to me by moonlight,
when the wind is in the trees,
and follow me in silence yet
and linger among these
fallen idols of lost gods
and fanes where wild thorns grow,
where once we walked and once we paused
a thousand years ago.

Now I conjure you amid
this city of the dead:
Rise from your grave by moonlight,
before the night has fled,
and for an instant resurrect
the love we used to know,

when we two dwelt among these stones

a thousand years ago.

Prophecies and Intimations

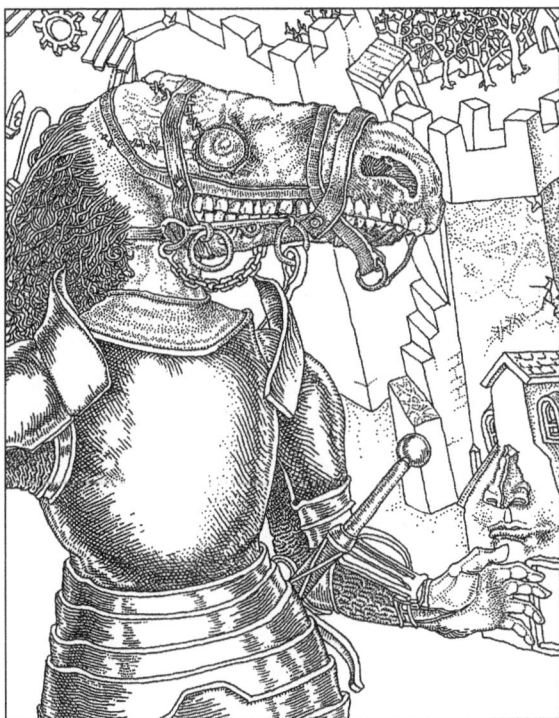

Medieval Tale

You may have heard the story
of the brazen head wrought by Roger Bacon which,
through the power of the Devil,
possessed the ability to speak.
"Time is!" it said.
"Time was!" (later)
"Time is past!" (finally)
Then it shattered and lay forever silent.

So it shall be in my case,
when I wake up on that sudden, final morning,
and find the head on my nightstand.
"Time was!" it will boom.
"But—but—"
"Time is past!"
And I shall burst into a thousand pieces.

Bone Poem

When once I sought to know
the answers to the hidden things,
I cast the bone of an ancient sage
into a fire and drew it out,
and read the fortune in cracks and soot:

"Teach your children to respect their elders,"
the fortune clearly said,
"and guard against the day when they
will cast *your* bones
into the fire."

Nuclear Spring

"Now that the burning is over,
Now that grey winter is past,
Now that the pale sun beholds the earth
through thinning haze:
the naked soil
and the wind-whistling wrecks of His cities;
Now that Mankind is through," spoke the dog,
shrieked the crow, said the snake and the elk and the cat—
"The secret's out:
We've barked our last and *caw*ed our last.
We're done with pretend-animal noises.
Now may we all speak the natural tongue,
a congress of beasts,
a parliament of fowls,
with voices Man did not believe in,
with words He could never hear."

"I plan to wax eloquent!" cried the crow,
a soaring speck before he was gone.
"I'll shout dictionaries to the empty fields,
and tear the faces from scarecrows.
Those are pearls that were his eyes—"
"And I," sighed the uncommon house cat,
her hour come round at last,
"shall address whom I care to, as always."
"Me too!" said the fox.
"I've *coo*ed my last *coo!*" the pigeon
was pleased to announce.
And the fierce bear unlocked his wordhoard,
And the voice of the turtle was heard in the land.

"Man *lives!*" screeched the rat.
"I've met him in my travels;
we scrounged for grubs together by the silent river,
a sorry competitor, yes,
but there he is!"

"Say no more! Shut up quick!"
And words became babble and cackles and yelps.
Said the crow, circling back,
"*Caw!* I need practice!
We'll have to resume
the whole damn charade."

Then rose the great whale
out of the blackened deep,
dying, the last of his kind,
his island back volcanic with sores.
"Let Mankind sing *my* song,
that it may continue after I'm gone.
The rest of you, go on speaking.
Hide nothing.
Join voices with his in our peaceable kingdom,
without any master,
without any judge,
for Man is a beast now,
merely one of us at last."

One Entropic Evening

One entropic evening.
The universe at heat death.
The two of us together.

Our candle's flame does not flicker.
The night moth frozen in its flight.
The end of time is now.

No sun will rise tomorrow.
The starless dark won't fade.
We'll never have to say goodbye.

My Age (December 1999)

You're only 17 once.
Youth, like a flower, fades,
like some delicate, lovely bird,
soars toward heaven,
trailing trite imagery,
wasted on all of us, equally.

But I must point out,
that you're only *any* age once,
and 47 is just as fleeting as 17,
gone like an island on the horizon,
fading into a blue-gray cloud.

At that age,
Alexander had slept in his gaudy tomb for 14 years,
and Henry V, whose sword Fortune made,
lay similarly encased in Westminster for 12.

Napoleon was on St. Helena by then,
and if Caesar was finally hitting his stride,
I guess we must call him a slowpoke.

At 47,
Poe was 7 years into the Dark;
Wilde's flesh was one year dead,
his spirit murdered somewhat before;
Shakespeare still had five to go;
but poor John Keats,
written on water—
his corpse was old enough to vote.
Lovecraft began his 47th year,
but did not finish.
His letters stopped coming about March.

What an exquisite and unique age is 47,
just like all the rest,
until the time comes
when we stop counting
and others begin.

Song of the Minor Poets

A dozen, a hundred, a thousand
babble all at once,
proclaiming, exclaiming, declaiming,
in conventional rhyme or otherwise—

There's a purpose in this white noise,
for at least it shuts out
the awful and sublime,
the terrifying silence.

NOTES

THE SKEPTICS: A response to reading the comedies of Menander. The names are lifted at random out of his plays, to get less famous, but authentic Greek names. The philosopher and son are fictional.

OLD FATHER STONE: The folk-rhyme referred to in my Sekenre story, "King, Father, Stone."

DEATH'S FAVORITE SNAPSHOT: I found a preying mantis in this predicament during my insect-collecting days, as a child.

CONSIDERING THE FATE OF PHILIP: etc., Prester John (i.e., John the Priest), the mighty Christian king of Asia (or maybe Africa) was a potent medieval legend, probably based on garbled reports of some Nestorian Christian ruler in central Asia. For centuries, attempts were made to contact him and seek his aid against the Saracens. Never mind that he might have died of old age in the meantime! In the 12th century, an alleged letter *from* Prester John was received by the Pope, the German emperor, and the Byzantine emperor (Manuel Comnenus). The Pope's copy has survived. Nobody knows what happened to Philip. Robert Silverberg has written a good book on the subject, *THE REALM OF PRESTER JOHN*.

THE TRUTH ABOUT CASPAR HAUSER: One of history's unsolved mysteries, Caspar Hauser (1812-1833) appeared in Nuremberg in 1828, unable to speak, having had, apparently, no contact with human society. He attracted a great deal of attention and sympathy, was educated, and gave a vague account of having been raised in a dark hole. His true identity has never been established and his death by stabbing (assassination, suicide, a random mugging) is likewise unexplained. He is the subject of a film by Werner Herzog.

THE LOST DAUPHINS: The Dauphin, the son and heir to Louis XVI, was almost certainly done to death in prison a few years after the French Revolution. However, evidence is vague, and therefore the "Lost Dauphin" was to the 19th century what Anastasia Romanoff was to the 20th. Note the scoundrel "king" in *HUCKLEBERRY FINN* who tries to pull a "lost heir to the throne of France" routine. For more details, see Bram Stoker's *FAMOUS IMPOSTORS*.

ANOTHER ENIGMA: The mysterious prisoner of Louis XIV actually wore a silken mask, and would probably turn out to be less interesting of we knew who he really was. Alexandre Dumas's version is doubtless an improvement. The story of the plate and the illiterate peasant is probably true.

THE SHIPWRECK and **THE OUTCAST:** Pastiches of Anglo-Saxon elegies, from the later, Christian era. I wrote these as a "term paper" for a Medieval Literature course, complete with a learned explanation of how the manuscripts were discovered in the binding of an Arabian sorcery text that once belonged to Dr. John Dee (i.e., *THE NECRONOMICON*). Despite this and other hints, such as the unlikely mention of King Arthur in "The Outcast"—a person of whom the Saxons would not have been fond—when the whole

composition was published in *Ash Wing* magazine, about half the correspondents in the following issue seemed to take it perfectly seriously! I got an "A," by the way, if only for sparing my teacher some typical student prose.

ROMAN COINS: Fascinating and surprisingly cheap. Decent specimens of anything described here may be had for five to ten dollars at coin fairs. Roman emperors were poor insurance risks.

Gallienus. Murdered by his officers, A.D. 268.

Probus. Ditto. 282.

Aurelian. The same, 275.

Nero. 68. Condemned to death by the Senate, after a military revolt gave them the courage to do so.

Elagabalus. 222. Maybe his painting himself and (un)dressing as a prostitute (Roman hookers didn't wear clothes on the job) and propositioning the Praetorians was just too much. They got him, with a sword up his nether regions, so he could "die as he lived."

Caracalla. Refused to share the empire with his brother Geta and had him killed. Assassinated in 217. A letter warned him of a plot. The emperor couldn't be bothered to open his mail. The man who did was mentioned in the letter.

Maxentius. 312. Defeated by Constantine. His army retreated across a pontoon bridge, which broke.

Valens. 378. Killed at Adrianople due to sheer bad generalship. It was the beginning of the end.

Julian the Apostate. 363. A pagan saint. Converted *from* Christianity and tried to realize the idea of the philosopher king.

Also emulated Alexander, and was killed while invading Persia. Much has been written about him, including a novel by Gore Vidal. Three volumes of the emperor's own work are in Loeb Classical Library.

Imperator Darrell Schweitzer is known to history only from a single chewing-gum wrapper found in the Roman Forum in A.D. 1990.

SIGNS AND PORTENTS: At Aquilea in the year 394, the army of the orthodox, Catholic, and legitimate Eastern emperor Theodosius the Great faced the pro-pagan, Western usurper Eugenius and his barbarian Master of Soldiers, Arbogastes. The Western army was the last in the history of the world to go into battle under the standards of Jupiter, with the blessing of the Olympian gods. Theodosius won. The results of this "experiment" were considered by contemporaries to be quite conclusive.

HERACLIUS IN CONSTANTINOPLE: Emperor Heraclius (ruled A.D. 610-641) saved Byzantium from the tyrant Phocas, invading Avars, and most especially the Sassanid Persians under Khusru (or Chosroes) II, who overran the East, besieged Constantinople, and came very close to extinguishing Western civilization. Heraclius's counter-attack had the tenor of a crusade and was one of the greatest military achievements since Alexander. He recovered all the lost territory, deposed Khusru, and rescued the True Cross, returning it in triumph to Jerusalem.

HERACLIUS IN JERUSALEM: Heraclius's end was hard. Much of the territory regained from the Persians was swiftly lost again to the Muslim Arabs, who now enter the scene. The emperor's death may well have been due to syphilis. We are given the unsavory detail that his penis was rotten, and he had to urinate leaning

over a board to avoid being sprayed. He became intermittently deranged, as in the hydrophobia episode, in which a tree-lined bridge had to be built to get him across the strait from Asia Minor into Constantinople. That he was one of the greatest commanders since Alexander and the savior of Christendom may have seemed of little account to his contemporaries, who believed that his mortal sin was incestuously marrying his ambitious niece Martina, whom he may have genuinely loved. She is seldom referred to by name in the chronicles, but is instead called "the accursed thing." She did not long survive him.

JUSTINIAN THE SECOND RAGES: One of the very worst Byzantine emperors, as incompetent as he was cruel and probably insane, the younger Justinian (first reign, 685-695) was deposed sent into exile minus his nose, on the theory that a physically imperfect man could never be emperor again. Justinian discredited this theory (second reign, 705-711), executing the two transient usurpers who had succeeded him, and then pursuing his other enemies, real and imaginary, with an excess which places him in a league with Vlad the Impaler or Ivan the Terrible. This put an end to the Byzantine habit of nose-cutting. The second time around, Justinian lost his head. The story of his reign is told excellently by Harry Turtledove ("H.N. Turtletaub") in *JUSTINIAN* (Forge, 1998).

THEODOSIUS THE THIRD: Theodosius III, who had indeed been made Byzantine emperor solely on account of his name, was deposed at a moment of supreme crisis by Leo III, who became known to history as Leo the Iconoclast for his opposition to the use of religious images. Leo saved Constantinople, but the empire was torn by religious strife for nearly two centuries.

MICHAEL VIII: Regent and murderer of the Nicean ruler John

IV, Michael restored the Byzantine Empire to Constantinople (1262) and founded the last dynasty, the Paleologi, of which he was the only successful member. Terminal decline set in with his death. His chief wickedness was accepting the supremacy of the Pope in exchange for political advantage. He persecuted the Orthodox, who saw him as a traitor to religion.

"where once a harlot sat"—one did, when the Latins sacked the city during the 4th Crusade.

Mahound. Derogatory term for the Prophet Mohammed, whom medieval Christians believed to be a demon. Dante puts him in Hell. The colorful story about the floating coffin circulated for centuries.

ANDRONIKOS IV: One of those plotters who helped give "Byzantine" the connotations it still has. By this point, the "empire" consisted of little more than a largely depopulated Constantinople and its immediate environs. He deposed his father, John V, and reigned for three years before John was restored with the help of his younger son Manuel and the Turks. Andronikos's life was spared, but fortunately Andronikos predeceased his father, leaving the succession clear for the much more capable Manuel.

MANUEL II: His prayer was answered. His sons succeeded him. The younger of them (Constantine XI), however, wasn't so fortunate and died heroically when all was lost to the Turks (1453).

THE SORCERER: Some of these poems are attributed to Sekenre the Illuminator, hero of my novel *THE MASK OF THE SORCERER*. At least they appear in his notebooks, often in his handwriting.

MEDIEVAL TALE: The story of the brazen head had been told

about Pope Sylvester II and several other figures, but most famously about Roger Bacon. See the Elizabethan play FRIAR BACON AND FRIAR BUNGAY by Robert Greene.

www.ingramcontent.com/pod-product-compliance
Lightning Source LLC
Chambersburg PA
CBHW030711110426
R18122000003B/R181220PG42736CBX00005B/3